This Orchard
book belongs to

_____

_____

For Becca and her new baby

Visit Catherine and Laurence Anholt's website at
www.anholt.co.uk

ORCHARD BOOKS

338 Euston Road, London NWI 3BH

Orchard Books Australia

Hachette Children's Books

Level I7/207 Kent Street, Sydney, NSW 2000

First published in hardback in Great Britain in 2012

First paperback publication in 2013

ISBN 978 I 40831 436 4

Text © Laurence Anholt 2012

Illustrations © Catherine Anholt 2012

The rights of Laurence Anholt to be identified as the author
and Catherine Anholt to be identified as the illustrator of this
work have been asserted by them in accordance with the
Copyright, Designs and Patents Act, 1988.

A CIP catalogue record for this book
is available from the British Library.

I 3 5 7 9 I0 8 6 4 2

Printed in China

Orchard Books is a division of Hachette Children's Books,
an Hachette UK company,

www.hachette.co.uk

BABIES, BABIES, BABIES!

Catherine and Laurence Anholt

ORCHARD

Here are the babies . . .

Cute baby,

cosy baby,

busy baby,

dozy baby,

noisy baby,   neat baby,   smelly baby,   sweet baby.

Can you find the funny baby bunny
through the book?

Babies love FOOD

Beans,

bread,

bananas,

salad,

spaghetti,

sultanas,

cherries,

chocolate,

cheese,

pasta,

pancakes,

peas,

fish,

fruit,

fries,

pizza,

potato,

pies,

radish,

rhubarb,

rice,

spinach,

sausage,

spice.

Babies love COLOURS

A fast blue car,

a sparkly silver star,

a green noisy parrot,

a tasty orange carrot,

a pretty pink rose,

a round red nose,

a bright yellow sun,

colours can be fun!

Babies love ANIMALS

Dogs who bark,
(WOOF WOOF!)

owls in the dark,
(TOO WOO!)

lions that roar,
(Ra-aww!)

bears who snore,
(Zzzzz!)

a pig in his house,
(oink oink!)

a tiny squeaky mouse,
(sque-ek squeak!)

a cat who likes to play,
(MIAO-OW!)

a horse eating hay,
(NE-EIGH!)

a monkey with a tail,
(**OO-OO-OO!**)

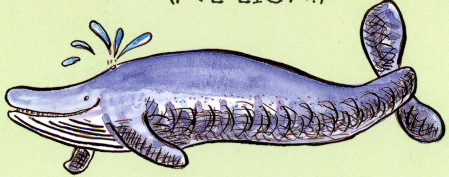

a great big whale,
(**splash!**)

elephants with trunks,
(**WAR-ROO!**)

stinky smelly skunks,
(POOH!)

a busy buzzy bee,
(bzzzz!)

someone hiding in a tree.
(Sshh!)

Babies love CLOTHES

Lots of baby clothes
Hanging up in rows.

Scarf, socks, suits,

bibs, bows, boots,

swimsuit,   sweater,   skirt,

shoes,   shorts,   shirt.

 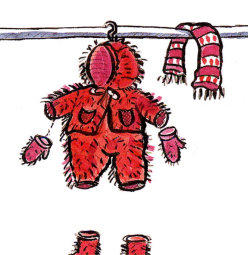 

 Clothes that go together,
clothes for every weather.

Babies love THE SEASIDE

Kites in the sky,

birds flying by,

a ball and a bat,

a baby in a hat,

air beds that float,

playing in a boat,

a bucket and spade,

a picnic in the shade.

Babies love MUMS and DADS

Feeding, reading,

tugging, hugging,

swaying, playing,

brushing, rushing,

talking, walking,   fixing, mixing,

caring, sharing,   peeping, sleeping.

Babies love GOING FAST

Get ready, get steady, let's GO!
Through the wind and the snow ~

in a powerboat,

police car,

or pram,

in a taxi,

a tugboat,

a tram,

in a truck, or a tractor, or train,

in a coach, or a cart, or a crane,

in a buggy, a bus, or balloon.

In a rocket, let's zoom to the moon!

Babies love PLAYING

You can **BANG** with saucepans and sticks,

you can build with play dough or bricks,

this dolly has lovely long hair,

make a house with a table or chair,

you can **splash** with water and boats,

you can dress up in costumes and coats,

make a picture with
crayons and glue,

this dinosaur
lives in a zoo,

you can run round the
room on a scooter,

and make LOTS OF
NOISE with a tooter,

these babies are
pretending to cook,

but the best toy of all
is a book!

Babies love NEW THINGS

This baby is learning
to walk,

this baby is learning
to talk,

this baby can make
lots of noise,

these babies can play
with their toys,

this baby's new tooth
is all white,

this baby can sleep
through the night,

these babies can sit
on their own,

just look how these
babies have grown!

Babies love LAUGHING

Tickle,

tumble,

roll about,

roly~poly,

dance,

and shout,

clap,

and sing,

and peek~a~boo,

little baby, I love you!

Babies love CUDDLE TIME

Up the stairs

to wash our
hair,

splash the
bubbles everywhere,

brush our teeth,

rub us dry,

babies love
a lullaby.

Pyjamas on and into bed,
look at all the books we've read,

even mummies can't help yawning,
we'll see these babies in the morning.

Squeeze us tight, switch off the light,
babies love to kiss GOODNIGHT.
Sleep tight, funny bunny!